Earth and Moon

BY FRED AND JEANNE BIDDULPH

The earth.

Is the earth flat?

No,
the earth is round like a ball.

The moon.

The moon is round like a ball, too.

What makes daylight on the earth?

The sun makes the daylight.
The sun shines on the earth.

What makes the light on the moon?

The sun makes the moon shine.

We can see the moon
in the day and at night
because the sun shines on it.

People live on the earth.
Millions and millions of people
live here.

People do not live on the moon.
There is no man in the moon, either.
The shapes you can see
are the mountains and plains
of the moon.

Why is the sky blue on Earth?

The sky is blue
because the sun shines on the air
above the earth.

Why is the sky black on the moon?

The sky on the moon is black
because there is no air
on the moon.

There is no air on the moon,
and there is no water.
The moon has no wind
and no clouds.

The earth has air.
It has water and wind
and clouds.

The moon

The earth

The earth is round.
The moon is round.
The earth gets light from the sun.
The moon gets light from the sun.

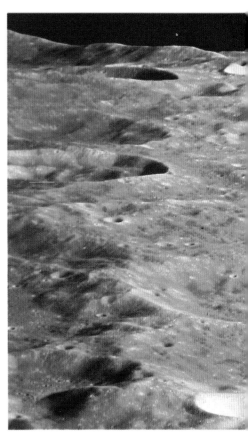

The earth has a blue sky.
The moon has a black sky.
The earth has air, water, and wind.
The moon has no air, no wind,
and no water.
The earth has people living on it.
No one lives on the moon.